Birds

KINGFISHER

a Houghton Mifflin Company imprint
222 Berkeley Street
Boston, Massachusetts 02116
www.houghtonmifflinbooks.com

First published in 2003
2 4 6 8 10 9 7 5 3 1

1TR/0503/PROSP/RNB(RNB)/140MA

LIBRARY OF CONGRESS CATALOGING-IN-PUBLICATION DATA
has been applied for.

ISBN 0-7534-5617-6

Senior editor: Belinda Weber
Coordinating editor: Stephanie Pliakas
Designer: Joanne Brown
Picture manager: Cee Weston-Baker
Picture researchers: Joanne Brown, Rachael Swann
Illustrations: Steve Weston
DTP manager: Nicky Studdart
DTP operator: Primrose Burton
Artwork archivists: Wendy Allison, Jenny Lord
Senior production controller: Nancy Roberts
Indexer: Chris Bernstein

Printed in China

Acknowledgments
The Publisher would like to thank the following for permission to reproduce their material. Every care has been taken
to trace copyright holders. However, if there have been unintentional omissions or failure to trace copyright holders,
we apologize and will, if informed, endeavor to make corrections in any future edition.
b = bottom, c = center, l = left, t = top, r = right

Photographs: *cover:* Ardea; 6-7 Corbis; 8b Corbis; 8-9 Getty Images; 9b Nature Picture Library (Nature);
10t Getty Images; 10-11 Natural History Picture Agency (NHPA); 11b Nature; 12 Bruce Coleman; 13t
Getty Images; 13b Bruce Coleman; 14b Corbis; 14-15 NHPA; 15b Nature; 16t Ardea; 16-17 NHPA; 17b Nature;
18 Bruce Coleman; 19t Getty Images; 19c Corbis; 19b Corbis; 20-21 Still Pictures; 21c Ardea; 21b Still Pictures;
22-23 Corbis; 23 Nature; 24 Corbis; 25tl NHPA; 25b Getty Images; 26bl Corbis; 26-27 Corbis; 29 Getty Images;
30 Corbis; 31all Getty Images; 32-33 Getty Images; 33t Nature; 33b Getty Images; 36b Getty Images; 36-37 National
Geographic Images Collection; 37t NHPA; 38b Corbis; 38cr Bruce Coleman; 39t Associated Press; 39b Nature;
40 NHPA; 41t NHPA; 41b Frank Lane Picture Agency; 46l Ardea; 46r Corbis; 47l Ardea; 47r Corbis

Commissioned photography on pages 42–45 by Andy Crawford.
Thank you to models Lewis Manu, Daniel Newton, Lucy Newton, Nikolas Omilana, and Olivia Omilana.

Kingfisher Young Knowledge

Birds

Nicola Davies

KINGFISHER
BOSTON

Contents

What is a bird?

Birds are everywhere! You can see them in forests, deserts, seas, and cities. There are 9,000 different types, but every one has wings, a beak, feathers, and feet.

Feathers

Birds are the only animals that have feathers. Tail and wing feathers are stiff and strong, while body feathers are silky and soft.

Feet

All birds have scaly feet. They have four toes for perching or grabbing prey. Eagles have strong talons on their toes.

perching—*holding onto something with the feet*

Wings

Birds need wings and strong feathers in order to fly. The bald eagle has large, powerful wings that let it soar and dive fast to catch its prey.

Beak

Birds do not have teeth to bite or chew. Instead they have beaks to grab whole food or to peck it into pieces. Every bird has the right shaped beak for the type of food it eats.

prey—an animal that is eaten by other animals

Flying made easy

Birds are good at flying because their bodies are made for it. Their bones are hollow and light, and they have big muscles to beat their wings up and down.

Light as a feather

A bird's skeleton weighs less than all of its feathers, so it can fly easily.

Safety first

These guillemots have found a safe place to nest high up on a cliff top. Flying means they can reach places like this, but their predators cannot.

Long-distance flights

The Arctic tern is the champion long-distance flyer. It flies almst 25,000 miles every year looking for food and places to nest.

Fast food

There are so many more places to eat when you can fly . . . grab some fruit from a treetop, catch some fish from the sea, or snatch a juicy insect right out of the air, as this bee eater has done.

predators—*animals that hunt and eat other animals*

Ways of flying

Every type of bird has a different way of flying, so they all have different shaped wings. Short wings are good for fast flapping, and long wings help with gliding.

Up, up . . .

Taking off is very hard work! This dove has to jump up from the ground or from a perch and then start flapping hard in order to go higher and faster.

. . . and away!

As the dove moves forward the air rushing under its wings helps hold it up, so it does not have to flap as hard.

hover—to stay in one place by beating the wings very fast

Flapping around

Hummingbirds have short wings that can flap very fast, so they can hover in the air.

Hanging around

Vultures have long, broad wings that catch the air, so they can glide all day and hardly need to flap at all.

glide—to fly with wings out without flapping

Birds on the ground

Not all birds can fly. Some are too big, some use their wings for swimming instead, and some can find food and safety without flying.

Big bird

An ostrich can weigh more than a person. It is too heavy to fly, but it can run away from danger at speeds of 45 miles per hour.

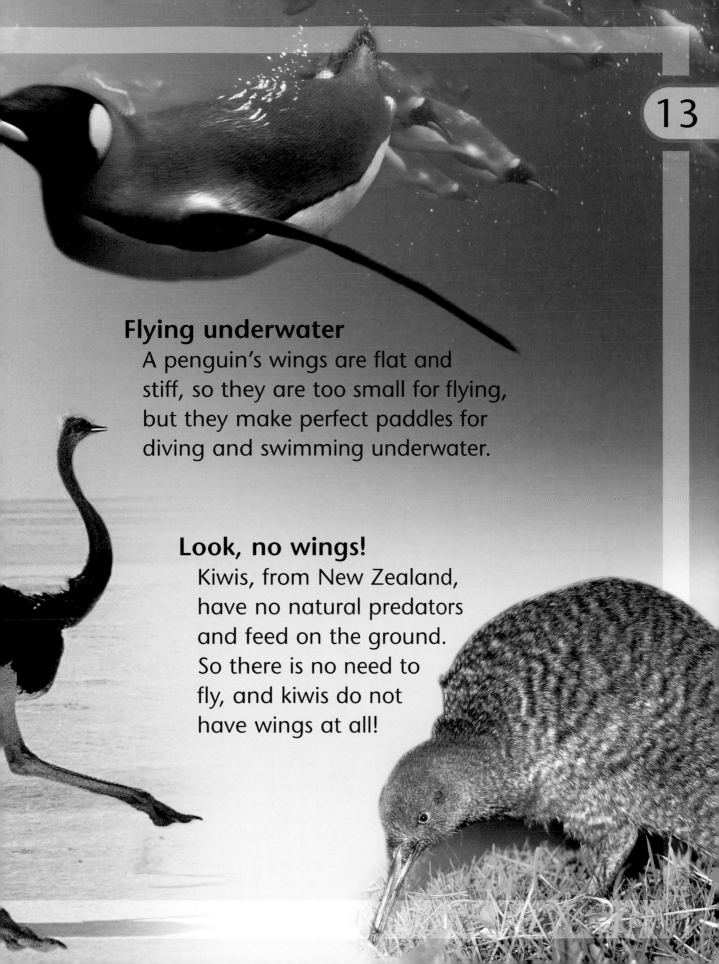

Flying underwater

A penguin's wings are flat and stiff, so they are too small for flying, but they make perfect paddles for diving and swimming underwater.

Look, no wings!

Kiwis, from New Zealand, have no natural predators and feed on the ground. So there is no need to fly, and kiwis do not have wings at all!

Hardworking feathers

Birds could not fly without feathers, but feathers do other jobs too. They keep birds warm, hide them from enemies, and help them communicate with their friends.

Hiding in the summer

It is always hard for predators to find a ptarmigan in the summer because it has dark feathers to blend in with summer plants.

communicate—to make other animals understand your message

Signal feathers

Macaws have brightly colored feathers so that they can find each other among the thick leaves of the treetops.

Hiding in the winter

But in the winter the ptarmigan stays hidden by growing white feathers to match the snow.

Fantastic feet

blue-footed booby

Birds' feet are made of four long toes, and are covered in tough, scaly skin. Birds can do a lot more with their feet than just standing, walking, or running. They use them for climbing, gripping, swimming, and even for saying hello!

Feet for swimming

Many waterbirds have webbed feet that act as paddles when swimming. The blue-footed booby also waves its brightly colored feet at its mate to say "hello"!

webbed feet—*feet with skin stretched between the toes*

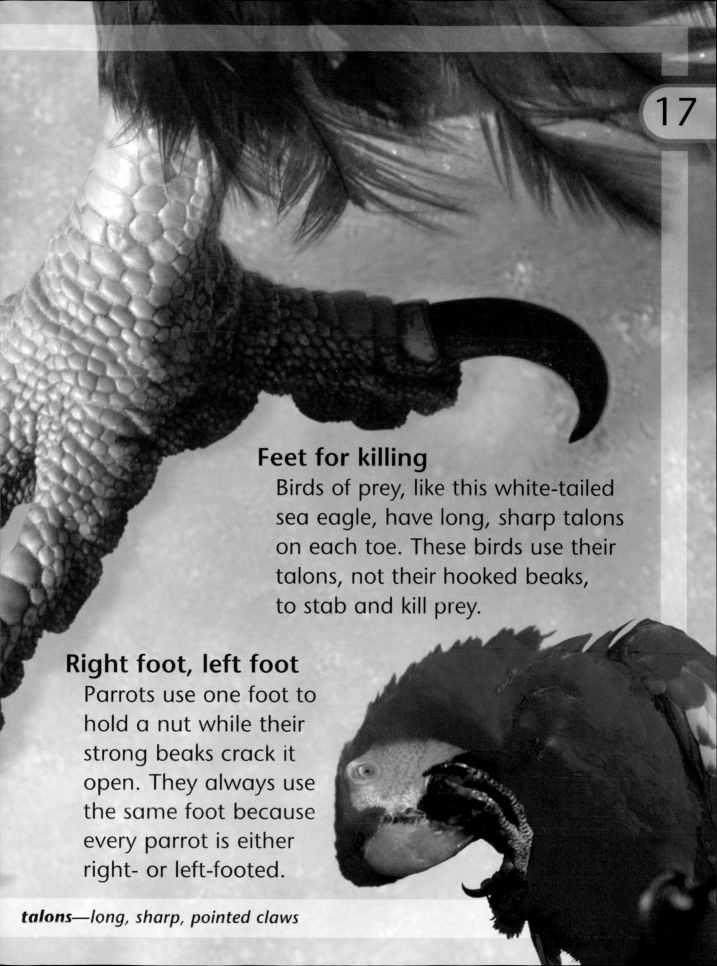

Feet for killing

Birds of prey, like this white-tailed sea eagle, have long, sharp talons on each toe. These birds use their talons, not their hooked beaks, to stab and kill prey.

Right foot, left foot

Parrots use one foot to hold a nut while their strong beaks crack it open. They always use the same foot because every parrot is either right- or left-footed.

talons—long, sharp, pointed claws

Breathtaking beaks

A beak is like a bird's toolbox. Every bird has a beak that gives it the right tools to help it find its food and survive.

Deep-down dinners

Curlews eat creatures like worms and snails. Their beaks can reach deep into the mud and grab prey that other birds cannot get. But their delicate beaks are just as good at picking tiny creatures from the surface of the mud—two tools in one beak!

Fishhooks . . . and showing off!

Puffin beaks have little spines inside of them to hold onto slippery fish—and the bright colors send messages to other puffins.

Huge . . . but not heavy

A toucan's bill is long and bright but is also very light because it is hollow.

Tricky tweezers

Pinecones are tough to open. Only a crossbill's beak can do the job and then pick out the small, flat, juicy seeds from inside.

bill—*another word for beak*

Super senses

Birds can use their senses—sight, hearing, touch, taste, and smell—to find out about the world around them. But just like humans, their most important senses are sight and hearing.

Invisible ears

An owl's ears are small holes hidden by feathers. But they are so good at hearing that the owl can find a tiny mouse in the dark just by using the sound around it.

Seeing rainbows

Birds see in color like we do. These lorikeets eat flowers, so color helps them find their food among the green leaves.

I spy

Birds of prey, such as this kestrel, have eyes that can see three times better than humans' eyes. They can spot tiny prey on the ground while they are flying high up above.

High-speed hunter

The peregrine falcon is the fastest and most deadly hunter on Earth. It can fly at up to 150 miles per hour, and its whole body is designed for speed and killing.

Tools for the job
Peregrines have very sharp eyesight for spotting prey, daggerlike talons for grabbing prey, and a hooked beak for tearing flesh into bite-sized pieces.

Stooping for speed . . .

Peregrine wings are pointed and narrow for fast flying, but for top speeds they fold their wings and dive down in a "stoop."

. . . and for killing

Stooping is how peregrines catch almost all of their prey. They stoop on flying birds, hitting them with their talons at more than 99 miles per hour.

stooping—when a bird folds its wings and dives through the air

Finding love

When a male bird wants to find a mate, he shows off with a special display. Every type of bird has a different display. Some birds dance and some sing, but they all say the same thing: "I'm fantastic—be my mate!"

Talking toes

Male blue-footed boobies do not have brightly colored feathers, so they wave their blue feet at the female boobies until one waves back!

display—when male and female birds "talk" with special calls and movements

Beautiful building

The male satin bowerbird builds a twig bower and decorates it with blue pebbles, shells, and flowers so that a female will notice him. He will even use human garbage— as long as it is blue!

Dancing cranes

Male and female cranes get to know each other by dancing, flapping their wings, and bobbing their heads to the sounds of their own calls.

bower—*an arch made of twigs*

Building a home

Birds are amazing builders! They make nests of all sizes and shapes to keep their eggs and babies safe from bad weather and predators.

Stick mountain
Ospreys make their nest by piling sticks in a tree. The nest is too big and heavy to blow away and too high for any hungry predators to reach it.

Hang on!
Weaverbirds use grass to weave a ball-shaped nest with one tiny entrance hole. The nest dangles from a twig, so the only way in is by flying.

Tree houses
Hoopoes like hollow trees. They are secure and cozy and just need to be lined with grass and leaves to build a nest.

weave—to twist threads and grasses together

Life is egg-shaped!

All birds start life as an egg laid by their mother. The baby bird grows inside, fed by the yellow yolk and protected by the hard outer shell.

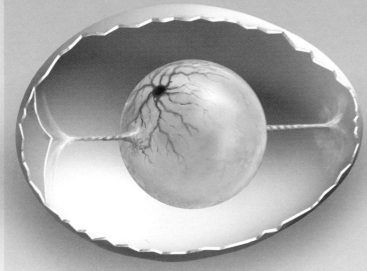

1. A warm start
Inside the egg the chick starts to grow as soon as incubation begins. It is just a tiny blob, but it changes very quickly.

2. Fast food
Food goes straight into the growing chick's stomach through the yolk, and its waste comes out into a small sac.

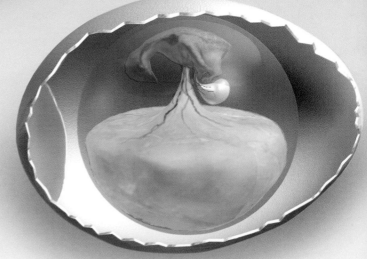

incubation—keeping an egg warm until it hatches

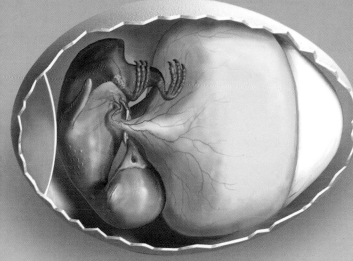

3. Getting into position

As the chick grows and uses up the yolk it moves to the rounded end of the egg. Its eyes and beak are already formed.

4. Ready for the world

The chick is so big that it fills the whole egg! When it is ready to hatch, the chick breaks the air sac and starts to breathe.

Mother hen

As soon as the chick starts breathing it calls to its mother, and she calls back. The birds soon learn to recognize each others' voices!

Feathers and fluff

Baby birds do not have real feathers. Some are covered in fluffy down when they hatch, but others are completely naked and grow fluffy feathers later.

Helpless hatchlings

When owlets hatch, they are blind, almost naked, and very helpless. These young owls have grown their first feathers.

Looking out
This baby chicken's eyes are open—even before it is out of the egg!

Fluffy and wet
It is covered in downy feathers that are still wet at first . . .

Ready to go
. . . but they soon dry. In a few hours the chick can leave the nest and follow its mother to look for food.

naked—*without feathers or hair*

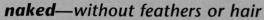
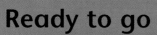

Raising babies

Raising baby birds is hard work! Bird parents have many different ways of giving their babies all the care and food they need.

It takes two . . .

Both albatross parents have to search hundreds of miles across oceans to find enough food for just one chick.

Cheating cuckoos

Cuckoos lay eggs in other birds' nests. The baby cuckoo hatches and pushes the other eggs out. The adult birds raise the cuckoo instead of their own babies.

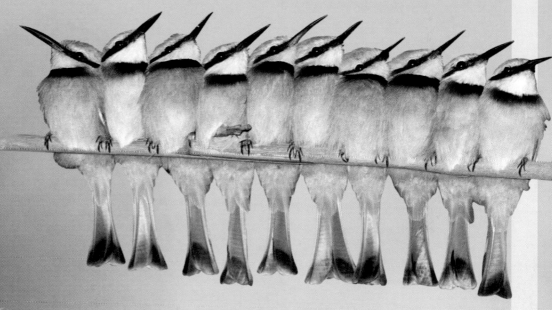

Teamwork

Mom, dad, and a whole team of older brothers and sisters work together to feed the bee eater babies. The more food they collect, the better chance the babies have of surviving.

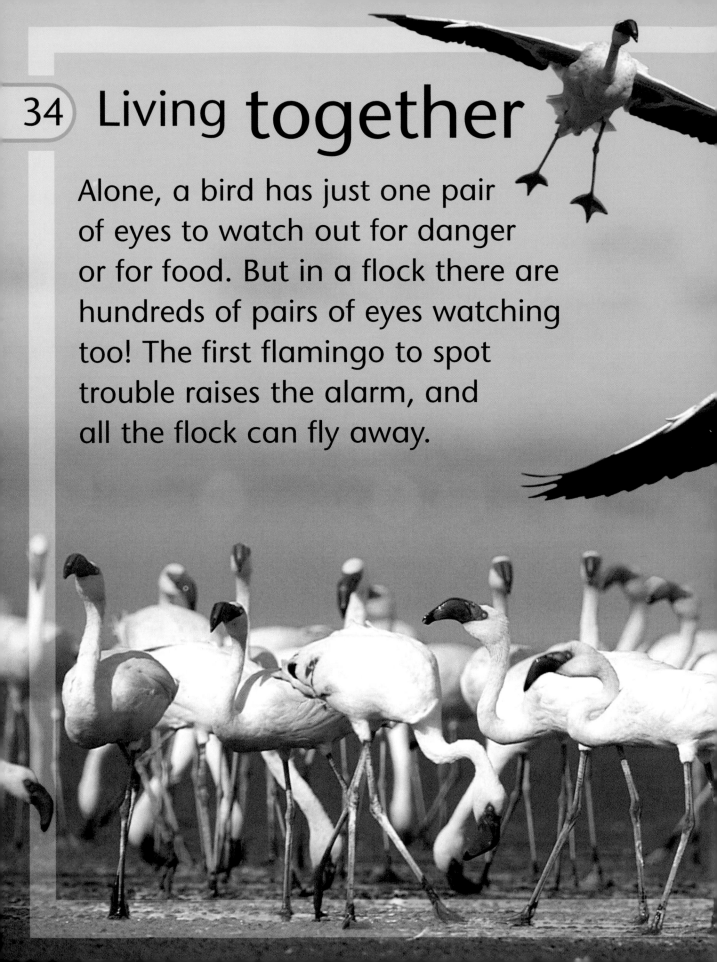

Living **together**

Alone, a bird has just one pair of eyes to watch out for danger or for food. But in a flock there are hundreds of pairs of eyes watching too! The first flamingo to spot trouble raises the alarm, and all the flock can fly away.

Party birds

Flamingoes feed and breed together in huge flocks of thousands of birds that can make whole lakes appear pink from far away.

Long-distance
travelers

Every fall millions of birds all over the world fly across seas and deserts and mountains to escape from the cold winter and to find warm weather and food. In the spring they fly all the way back again!

Finding the way

Geese fly in a "V" formation. This means that they can always see the bird in front that is leading the way.

"V" formation—making an arrow pattern in the sk

Fat for flying

At migration time birds get fat to give them the energy they need for their journey.

Safety in numbers

Birds gather together before migration and travel in large flocks. This means that they all leave at the right time and that no one gets lost!

migration—*making the same journey every year at the same season*

Birds in danger

People are bad news for birds. Hundreds of birds are in danger of becoming extinct because of what we have done. But it is not too late to make things better.

Pet parrots

Wild parrots are sometimes sold as pets. We can stop this by never buying birds that have been taken from the wild.

Bathing birds

Oil spills kill millions of seabirds. Many birds can be saved by washing them and keeping them safe and warm until their feathers have dried.

extinct—*none left alive anywhere on Earth*

Condors going up!

Rare Californian condors almost became extinct. In 1987 there were only 22 Californian condors left in the world. Then they were bred in zoos and put back in the wild. Now there are almost 200!

Losing their homes

The forests where Philippine eagles live are being cut down. But local people are learning how to protect the birds and their forest homes.

The secret life of birds

There are many things that we do not know about birds. Scientists have developed different ways of finding out more about their mysterious lives.

Penguin radio

The radio tag on this Adelie penguin's back sends out a signal that tells scientists how far it travels and how deep it dives to find its food.

radio tag—a device that sends out invisble signals that can travel long distances

Give me a ring!

The ring being put on this bird's leg carries a unique number—so the bird can be tracked throughout its life to find out how long it lives.

Who's who?

Colored rings on this rare wrybill's legs help us tell it apart from other wrybills. Scientists can figure out how many of these birds are left and find ways to help protect them.

unique—the only one

42 Make a bird book

Make your own bird scrapbook
It is fun to keep a scrapbook about all of the different types of birds you see. You can write down what they look like, where you saw them, and what time of year it was. All of these things will help you understand birds better.

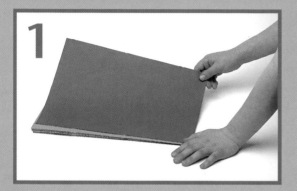

Collect some sheets of different colored plain paper. If necessary, trim the pages so that they are all about the same size.

You will need
- Colored paper
- Hole punch
- Ribbon or string
- Candy wrappers
- Feathers
- Sequins
- Wrapping paper
- Orange peel
- Paintbrush
- Scissors and glue
- Cardboard or pieces of plastic

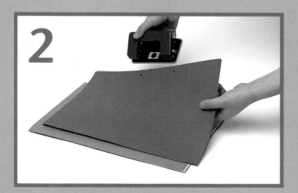

Being careful to keep your fingers out of the way, punch holes in the pages of your book. Make sure that all of the holes line up.

Thread some brightly colored ribbon or string through all of the pages to keep them together. Leave the ends at the front.

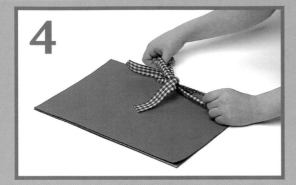

Tie the ends of the ribbon together in a loose bow. This will mean that the pages can turn more easily without ripping.

Draw a picture of a bird on the front of your book. Think about the different colors and textures of the materials you have gathered and make a collage. The beak is hard, so cardboard or plastic would be good. Birds' feet are scaly, so dried orange peel or sequins will give the right texture.

Collect feathers, candy wrappers, and wrapping paper to decorate the front of your book. Add dried orange peel for texture.

44 Feed the birds

Make a bird table

Birds make welcome visitors to any home. Encourage local birds to dine at this easy-to-make bird table.

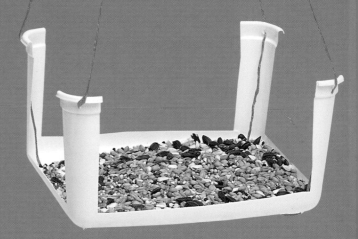

1

Very carefully, cut the sides out of a clean, empty ice cream carton. Leave wide "legs" of plastic at each corner.

You will need
- Ice cream carton
- Scissors
- Modeling clay
- Compass
- String
- Birdseed

2

Using a compass, make a hole near the top and the base of each leg. Use a lump of modeling clay to protect your hands.

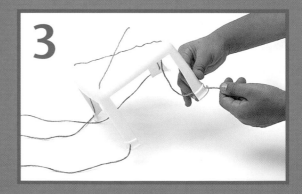

3

Thread the string through the holes, making a cross on the bottom and leaving long ends. You can tie the ends over a branch to hang your table. Put in lots of birdseed and watch for visitors.

Seedcake treat

Every bird has its favorite food, but this bird cake is a treat many will enjoy.

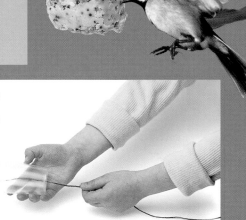

You will need
- Plastic cup
- String or wire
- Scissors
- Modeling clay
- Cooking pan
- Wooden spoon
- Lard or butter
- Birdseed

Make a hole in the bottom of a plastic cup, protecting your hands with a ball of modeling clay. Thread the string or wire through.

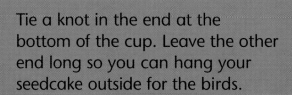

Tie a knot in the end at the bottom of the cup. Leave the other end long so you can hang your seedcake outside for the birds.

Ask an adult to melt some lard or butter in a cooking pan and carefully stir in the seeds. Fill the cup with the mixture, keeping the string free.

Once the cake has set carefully cut away the cup. Now you can hang the cake outside for the birds to feast on.

46 Using nest boxes

Different homes for different birds

Each type of bird has its favorite place to nest. So when you put up a nest box, make sure it is the right shape and size, and in the right place, for the birds in your area.

Ducks in trees

Black-bellied whistling ducks like to nest in holes in trees. Boxes attached to tree trunks are just as good!

Pretend it is a hole

Many small birds, like titmice, nest in tree holes. A box with a small entrance to keep out predators seems just like a tree hole to a titmouse.

Up on the roof
Storks like to nest in tall trees or on rooftops, but a special platform like this above the roof of a house is even better!

Treetop owls
Barn owls want to feel safe, high up in an old barn or in a tree hole. So this big nest box 16 feet up a wall is safe and sound.

Making the birds welcome

- Choose the right box for the birds you want to attract.
- Make sure it is firmly attached to a tree or wall.
- Check the box each year and replace any damaged parts.

- If you have to visit the box, do so quietly.
- Do not revisit your nest box once a family has adopted it.
- Remove old nests at the end of each season.

Index